DEDICATION:
TO THE TEACHERS IN OUR LIVES, FROM WHOM
WE HAVE NEEDED EVERY LESSON.

FINN the Frog Who Played the Violin

STORY AND PICTURES BY DAVID MARSHALL

STORYMAN BOOKS PUBLISHERS

Copyright © 2018 by David Marshall

All rights reserved. For information about permission to
reproduce selections from this book, Email:
DavidStoryman@gmail.com

www.storymanbooks.com

davidstoryman@gmail.com
http://www.storymanbooks.com

Library Congress Cataloging-in-Publication Data
Marshall, David
FINN The Frog Who Played The Violin
1. Juvenile Fiction 2. Bullying 3. Self Esteem 4. Leadership

ISBN 978-1-7322282-4-5

Printed in the United States of America

First Edition

Every night Finn would hop onto his lily pad and just as the sun was going down, Finn would begin to play his violin. He was good at it. Finn loved playing his violin. He was happiest when he was standing on his lily pad, playing music across the pond for all of the creatures to hear.

When Finn played, the dragonflies came out to hear his music. Even the fish would swim up from the bottom of the pond and lie just below the surface so they could feel the beautiful music as it vibrated through the water.

All of the other frogs would angrily gather around the pond because, after all, the very idea of a frog playing the violin was absurd. Everyone knows that this is not how a proper frog behaves.

Finn thought to himself, *Isn't it strange that even though they do not seem to like me playing my violin, they come out every night to listen to me play?*

Perhaps, he thought, *they enjoy my playing, or maybe, just maybe, they respect me for being brave enough to be who I am.*

The other creatures realized that the pond wouldn't mean anything without the music of Finn, but the other frogs just laughed and thought it was all just too ridiculous for a frog to play the violin.

From across the pond, one of the frogs in the crowd said, "If I were Finn, I would just leave and never come back." With that, all the frogs fell silent and just stared at Finn.

This gave Finn an idea.

The next night all the frogs came out to listen to Finn play his violin like they had countless nights before, and all the frogs gathered on the other side of the pond, just as they had countless nights before, except this time Finn wasn't there. "He must be late," said one of the frogs from the edge of the pond. So they waited, and waited, and waited.

Finn never came.

Finn didn't show up the next night, or the next night, or the night after that. Still, all of the frogs came out night after night to see if Finn would come back and play his music, but Finn never came. Soon the frogs were wondering where he went. Strangely, they missed Finn and realized the pond wasn't the same without Finn and his violin.

Finally, one night all the frogs had gathered around the pond, and they stood silently. They closed their eyes and hoped Finn would come back. The frogs promised that if Finn came back, just one more time, they would never criticize him again.

From deep in the middle of the gathering frogs, Finn quietly stood up, raised his violin and began to play! All the frogs were stunned, shocked, and couldn't believe their eyes!

While Finn kept playing, another frog stood up playing the saxophone! And then more frogs stood up, another playing a horn, then a trombone, and a trumpet! It was amazing that all the frogs were performing their song together. The music filled the pond like never before. They were happier than they had ever been.

The frogs got so caught up in playing their music that they didn't notice that Finn was gone. Out on the lily pad where he used to play was a piece of paper. One frog leaped out to the lily pad and picked up the note. As he started reading the note, his face dropped. He began to feel sad, but as he finished reading he looked out to all the frogs and the animals, and a big smile spread across his face.

The note read,

To all my friends, sister and brother frogs, you have come to appreciate your talents so much that you now can play your own song. It is time for me to leave our pond because there are so many others who have never learned the sound of their own song. Every time I play my violin, I will close my eyes and think of you all, and I will hear your beautiful song.

Love,
Finn

Color FINN

David Marshall is a children's book author and illustrator. David's children's stories carry life-giving, inspirational and meaningful messages. He believes that when kids read, they learn how and when to trust, dream and succeed. Storytelling helps children find a connection with their world, with their parents, teachers and with each other. Children face their challenges in many ways. David's goal is to use stories to help children meet those challenges in life.

You can reach David at DavidStoryman@gmail.com

Other Books by David Marshall

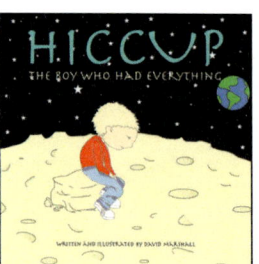

HICCUP
The Boy Who Had Everything
Hiccup is a boy who gets everything he asks for and soon learns that getting everything you want might not be what it is made out to be.

In this delightful story, the lessons illustrated will go a long way to help the whole family.

I Planted A Seed
Learning to say goodbye is one of the hardest lessons we face in life. Learning this natural part of life can be difficult and too often one we fear. But, it doesn't have to be a scary experience.

In this tale, a boy plants a seed and learns one of life's most valuable lessons. The most difficult times in life, often hold the most precious gifts - when we learn how to see.

FINN
The Frog Who Played The Violin
FINN has an exceptional talent for playing the violin, but his most unique ability is what he is about to give to others.

Finn, the violin-playing frog, always knew who he was and what his talents were. But when all the other frogs try to tease him and discourage him, will FINN compromise his values and dreams?

I Learned Something Today
A story about bullying. Until the bully's heart changes, bullying is going to be with us. Until we start teaching emotional wellness at the elementary school level, there will be angry children moving through their childhoods, leaving pain and heartache in their wake.

While every victim's story must be told, every bully needs to be aware of the very real devastation and seriousness of their actions.

I just want to be normal, that's all.

Today's children often face the safety of conformance and the risks of independence. It's a choice that can mean the difference between life – and of a lifetime. Children often feel like they don't fit in and either struggle for recognition or grow quiet and withdraw. This humorous story helps kids understand that it is our differences that are often our biggest assets and learning to recognize what makes us different is what makes us unique and beautiful.

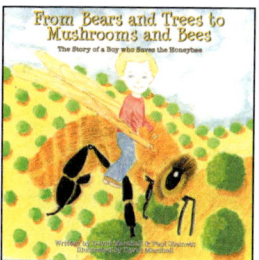

From Bears and Trees To Mushrooms and Bees

In this book, the main character Max is a boy whose curiosity leads him on a scientific path to solve a worldwide problem: Save the bees! The story underscores the complex inter-relationships of life cycles between bears, trees, mushrooms, bees, humans and much more.

David hopes this story will inspire your children to become Citizen Scientists. The message is that we need to protect this beautiful planet we call Earth, our home.

What Will I Become?

Children often desperately search for acceptance and success. Often undervaluing who they are and what they can do. Learning to have a healthy sense of self can be the most significant lesson a child can learn.

In, What Will I Become? Children learn that be happy in life starts with learning how to be happy with who you are.

ADDO The Story Of A Baby African Elephant

For a child, the frightening feelings of abandonment and loss are not easily explained. Today these experiences are labeled with clinical words too clinical for a child to understand or make the connection to the meaning of life. It's time for a different way of imagining this shared experience, and therefore a different way of helping children deal with it.

In ADDO David illustrates how a common disconcerting experience can be a treasured moment of transformation.

Visit Storyman Books at www.storymanbooks.com

Made in the USA
San Bernardino, CA
21 May 2018